WHOMP AND MOONSHIVER

BOA EDITIONS, LTD.:
NEW POETS OF AMERICA SERIES

WHOMP AND MOONSHIVER

Poems by Thomas Whitbread

Foreword by Richard Wilbur

BOA EDITIONS, LTD. • BROCKPORT NEW YORK • 1982

Grateful acknowledgement is made to the editors of the following publications in
which some of the poems, or earlier versions of them, originally appeared:
Approach: "Post Card from Esna, Egypt," "Shiloh," "Bee"; *The Carleton Miscellany:*
"Domestic Scene and One-Line Epilogue," "on a Painting by E. A. W. Teall," "On the
Popping Out of Eyes"; *The Georgia Reviw:* "Echo"; *Harper's Magazine:* "The Best
Place to Read Carlyle," "Shiloh: The Bloody Pond," "Analysis"; *The Idler:* "In Praise
of M. B. Tolson"; *Lucille Poetry Journal:* "Syracuse, Kansas, Summer '59," "Said from
Colorado," "End of a Winter Day," "Elegy Gorge," "Fun and Hope in Bristol, Eng-
land," "Saguaro," "Vignette," "Pearl Harbor, 1976: An Agony against Suicide"; *The
Massachusetts Review:* "Rites," "Guts," "Tact," "The Assertions"; *The New Review:*
"Lesson"; *Perspective:* "Bede," "Question," "Nearing a January"; *Poetry Northwest:*
"Leggiero," "Self-Lover," "Lie"; *Riata:* "Whomp and Moonshiver," "Wish"; *Shenan-
doah:* "Pochet Island"; *The Texas Observer:* "November in Texas," "Lime Town in
Texas," "Ranch Road 385"; *The Texas Quarterly:* "Love of Life," "Poor Death,"
"Dying Body," "The Circulation of the Lymph." "The Children's Snow" appeared
originally in *The New Yorker.* "An American Life," "Thomas Hardy," and "T. S.
Eliot," © by The New York Times Company. Reprinted by permission. "Sidney
Greenstreet, Late, Become Our Avatar" and "Janie's Sheet" originally appeared in
Quartet (Texas Writers' Special) Nos. 51-53, Summer-Fall-Winter 1975-76. "Love Son-
net," reprinted from SOUTHWEST *Review,* Winter 1967, copyright 1967 by South-
ern Methodist University Press. "Wood," "Beside the Sea, Ignorant Murderer," and
"Lake Windermere," July 10, 1967, © *The Virginia Quarterly Review.* "St. George,
Utah" first appeared in *Southwest Writers Anthology,* ed. Martin Shockley (Steck-
Vaugn Co., 1967). "November 25, 1963" first appeared in *Of Poetry and Power: Poems
Occasioned by the Presidency and by the Death of John F. Kennedy,* edd. Erwin A. Glikes
and Paul Schwaber (Basic Books, 1964). "Pochet Island" was reprinted in *The Ameri-
can Literary Anthology/1: The First Annual Collection of the Best from the Literary Maga-
zines* (Farrar, Straus & Giroux, 1968). "Pochet Island" and "Lesson" were reprinted in
East of America: A Selection of Cape Cod Poems, ed. John V. Hinshaw (The Chatham
Press, 1969). "T. S. Eliot" was reprinted in *The New York Times Book of Verse,* ed.
Thomas Lask (Macmillan, 1970). "November 25, 1963" and "Lake Windermere, July
10, 1967" were reprinted in *Poetry Amherst: A Sesquicentennial Anthology of Poems by
Alumni of Amherst College,* ed. Richard Aldridge (Amherst College Press, 1972).

Publication of this book made possible with the assistance of a grant from the Litera-
ture Program of The New York State Council on the Arts.
Designed and printed at the Visual Studies Workshop, Rochester, New York.
Typeset by Open Studio, Rhinebeck, New York.
Distributed by Writers & Books, 892 South Clinton Ave., Rochester, N.Y. 14620.

ISBN 0-918526-30-2 Cloth
       0-918526-31-0 Paper
Library of Congress # 82-071634

First Edition: October 1982

BOA Editions, Ltd.:
A. Poulin, Jr., Publisher
92 Park Avenue
Brockport, N.Y. 14420

CONTENTS

A CLEAR GLASS ON THE WORLD

The prevalence of a loose "naturalness" in contemporary
poetry has made the ordinary reader a poor critic when he
encounters meter, rhyme, and the like; he can't well distin-
guish the honest, functional use of such means from a frilly
and obtrusive formalism, and that's too bad. Still, it would
take a very ordinary reader to find a culpable artificiality in
Thomas Whitbread's poems. Their language has a supple
openness, as of an amiable and intelligent man talking; both in
its playfulness and in its gravity, it avoids the stagey; and it
easily enlists any suitable form in the pursuit and sharpening
of its point. On the few occasions when one feels a saliency of
"technique," there's good reason for it. Consider "Whomp
and Moonshiver," the title poem of this book. Its words move
in a rushed, jumbled, rackety way through wrenched con-
structions, ellipsis, and dropped punctuation; yet all the time
they are executing, for heaven's sake, a Petrarchan sonnet.
Milton and Hopkins, for their own expressive purposes, sub-
jected this most exacting form of the sonnet to violent strain.
Whitbread's ebullient straining of the form expresses a siding
with life's din and motion against dead fixity. In "Pearl Har-
bor, 1976," the first line is repeated, refrain-like, at regular

intervals, not for mere pattern's sake but to embody the poet's helpless urgency and to convey the bonding in his mind of Beethoven's music, the anniversary of the attack on Pearl Harbor, the death of a friend in a faraway desert, and the threatened suicide of another. "Elegy Gorge" is written in one long sentence, to stress the idea of precipitousness and to imitate a runaway anxiety. A comparable poem in Whitbread's first book, *Four Infinitives,* aims at a different effect: "Why I Eat at Caruso's" is also done in a single long sentence, not out of arbitrary virtuosity but (in part, at least) to express the poet's delight in a cluttered ensemble of kitsch and taxidermy.

Delight. That's what one thinks of first when Whitbread's work comes to mind. A casual glancer at *Four Infinitives* might take it for a nostalgic book centered upon the lost well-being of childhood, and indeed much of it is happily perceived with the senses of that "clear sensationalist," the child. I think of the delectable woods as one steps into them in "Summer Afternoon;" of the boy leaping on his bed and sliding down into it, in "Ubi Sunt;" of the splendid passing train seen from a high window in "Castling;" of the trusty handlebars of "Child on a Bicycle." And it's true that the child of that last poem would like to "stay a child," and pedal away from all distress. Nevertheless the poems straightforwardly acknowledge, as part of the poet's awareness and the child's as well, such things as fear, sadness, hatred, disillusion, change, and death. The child's self, in "The River," changes overnight; there are deaths and near-deaths even of the young; and age and death are "certain comings" for all. The poems admit, in short, the evidence which led Randall Jarrell to think of life in terms of losses, and to judge it a bad bargain; but Whitbread elects a different emphasis, knowing that "the mind can juggle memories" and so preserve what was good, can make from passing moments "a pattern permanent and fair."

Is this an Epicurean prudence which avoids, as in such a new poem as "Syracuse, Kansas," the lamentable west end of town? I think not. Though I discover in Whitbread's poems no theological imperatives to hope and rejoice, they have a seldom-shaken assurance that what is happy is most real, that one should maintain a mind reminiscent and expectant of joy, that people should "sow songs as they go to seed." There's a more decided personality in these poems than in most "confessional" writings, and the poet is onstage in most of them; nevertheless, the focus is seldom on himself as a peculiar being. He will not be his own hero, but he is quick to admire the good swimmer "smashingly slashing ahead," or the able man who will not hate those who envy him, or the medical student called to make his life "a love to be believed." He celebrates a "fine" drive on Ranch Road 385, a merging of human and natural peace at Windermere, good times in Maine or Bristol, and above all the mutual enjoyment and concern of friends. As a natural corollary, he regrets the stand-offish and superior, as in "Wish" and "Said from Colorado." The presence among us of a frankly humane and praiseful poet, for whom euphoria is a clear glass on the world, may sound too good to credit. Well, read "Pochet Island" and see if it doesn't ring true.

— Richard Wilbur

LOVE OF LIFE

The sun is going to go out.
   It just sank, and sends up its shoots,
   Yellowy orange, from what roots
The squashes know, the turnips doubt.

The haze becomes the dust, the dust
   Becomes the haze — clogged is the air — :
   Brushgrass and juniper impear
This landscape of dirt and stirred rust.

How shall we live, before we die?
   By taking Arizona snow
   Into our minds in April. So
We exercise a living eye.

The hazedust deepens, sage is soft,
   Saguaro blossom, and the sheen
   Of what we want and what we mean
Massachusetts in a hayer's loft.

POOR DEATH

Death cannot entertain the life,
Even if he exist, that I
Imagine, without any strife,
Clear eye looking into clear eye.

That is too much for Death, who needs
Windshield wipers on his glasses, to
Improve his ways of seeing you
And me, and others he misreads.

Death may yet understand, if he
Consent to let his tie to time
Dwindle, let spring meet his rime,
And come play tennis, just us three.

DYING BODY

As the body dies, how does its beauty live?
By accumulation of indignities.
Hitting its head on ceilings, making impossible
Golf shots over shafts of trees to greens
Unseen from tees? By giving up for lost
Accumulations? going on long journeys?
Stopping at signs? Historical Markers? Road-
side Rests? Observing observed principles
Of versification?
                            No.
                                    As the body
Dies, it requires strictest attention,
Nutriment, doctors, nurses,
Everyone who has given it harm,
Each person who has loved it,
All, arm-in-arm,
To keep it warm.

THE CIRCULATION OF THE LYMPH

Where can the hot blood go?
Nowhere, until the end
Of life. It makes its slow
   Way through its friend,

The body. When that dies,
The hot blood cools, then slows,
And stops. All its allies
   Give up their shows.

The liver says its name
Is inaccurate. The heart
Says "Eat me." Every part
   Proclaims the same

Except the lymph nodes, which
Led intersected flesh
To realize its mesh
   Was much too rich.

WHOMP AND MOONSHIVER

Whomp and moonshiver of salt surf on sand,
Beer cans, rocks, seawall: Galveston night vision
Anyseawhere hear- and seeable, incision
Cut into land, incessant dentist's hand
At drill, letless force, without countermand
Order thump order order thump intermission
Thump order thump thump thump order No Permission
For surfers Danger Deep Holes yet all how grand.

Palls the heart, yet how go on without? Within
Gyrates the heart, at such terrific. If
Heart is the essence of a humane being
And life love, let heart leap to share its thin
Pump with the din about against the stiff
Photograph that succeeds the act of seeing.

WISH

The train that carried Lincoln's corpse linked him
With all the people who brought lilacs to him.
It was a bandage for a wounded land.

The train that carried Eisenhower's corpse
Went guarded, fast as it could, mostly at night,
Pre-dawn engine change, West Virginia, the main contact.

The train that carried R. F. Kennedy's
Corpse was preceded by a shadow train
To draw the fire: itself turned murderer.

I wish for each of my friends, whether or not
He or she has any position, a very
Slow train that will stop many times, to let

The scheduled, the milky, the flagging, the anyhow
Human show to an earthbound man respect.

POCHET ISLAND

The ticks jumped on our legs as if we were dogs
As we walked to the beach through marsh-grass. Shaggily
We went, more shaggily each step. We stopped
Now and then to pick the ticks off. My dog Buff
Has similar, worse troubles, all the summer,
And has developed a stoic eye. We had
No such resource. We were glad to reach the sea.
After we swam, we walked back through more ticks
Picked off at intervals, to the house. I was
The outsider. The three others knew each other:
The husband, the wife, the husband's longtime friend.
Their talk was largely local. I sat in
Happily, though, since all three were nice, and I
Not unnice. We drank, ate, played Scrabble, then
Ran low on whiskey. We were on an island
Kerosene-lamped, a half-mile from the mainland, and
It was nine o'clock and raining. Therefore I
Volunteered, announced, insisted I would go
Provide. They got me into a sticky old
Two-piece rubber cement rainsuit, told me not
To go, gave me a flashlight, and I went.
Time was both fast and slow at once. I lost
An oar in the middle of the bay, said *no*
To panic, and with light and paddling found
It again. No trouble in returning. When
I got to the door with scotch and beer, she asked
Who I might be? what I was doing out
On a night like this? was I friend or foe? My host
The husband said he had worried. His old friend
Approved the provisions. We played on into
The middle night, while a clock went tock and tick.

Next day, hungover, before breakfast of
Tomato juice, eggs, coffee, coffee, coffee,
I walked out in the rain–drenched grass down through
Rain-bearing bushes to the bay, and stood
Against a fresh gale, which made anything
Feel right. When I walked up and back, we were
Four friends. Such happenings give worth to life.

SYRACUSE, KANSAS, SUMMER '59

An overnight stop. *Yes, there are cheaper motels*
On the west side of town, but you wouldn't. Oh.
No. We wouldn't.
                    Vegetable soup,
Pear, cottage cheese and lettuce leaf, liver
And onions, mashed potatoes, mashed squash, turnips,
Coffee, jello and cream — oh, and bread and butter
And jelly and soda crackers — what a meal
For ninety-five cents!
                    Eight o'clock. Too early
To go to bed. Exploring. In the square
Center of town, one block off US 50,
A sign, hand-crayoned: *BASEBALL GAME TONITE.*
Gas station: *one mile south.*
                    Worn wooden stands.
Asparagus stalks cauliflowering bulbs.
Players playing, one team uniformed, one dressed
Nine different ways. A voice: *Will the car parked*
Down the right field foul line please turn off your lights?
Thank you. Two balls, one strike. Groups of farmers
Sitting and talking and watching, overalled blue,
Eyed motley. High school sons and daughters here,
Then gone in a motor roar, then here again.
Trailer trucks on the highway near. Out far
In the unjudgeable distances, heat lightning.
The home team winning easily.
                    All's well
Here, all's breaded veal cutlet near
The heart.
          We only stayed one night.
We didn't get to know anyone at all.
Good motel, fine meal, American town baseball.
Fine. Driving west, we hardly saw the cheap
Indiscriminate anyone shacks as we hurried by.

SAID FROM COLORADO

Each Rocky Mount impends,
In its incredible exactitude,
Like a portending monarch among friends,
    One who eats food,

Then excuses himself
From, and above the left felt twitter, laughs
At human wars, at Ghibelline and Guelf,
    As wheat whose chaffs

Leave him by gravity.
Such a tremendous high effect imports
To granaries around it, granite. We
    Who may be sports,

Or diamonds slightly off
In perfect settings, surely understand
That we here, save each Godforsaking cough,
    Are in God's hand.

Those down there on the plains
Include our rejected cigarettes and brothers,
Our near-marriages, our former lives, loves, stains,
    Mirages, others.

END OF A WINTER DAY

Outside, the dark
Seems to come down like foggy snow
And then collect itself
In corrupted treetop chalices, then go

Down to the ground
And through the raw, compacted leaves
Into some socketed nest
Where the host, ancient, having given, receives.

ELEGY GORGE

Conceive a gorge, in it a waterfall,
Edged by dark rocks with clefts, in which put trees
Precarious, stern, clinging, and so tall
One wonders on their roots, and what disease
In the jaw of their stone sockets may set in
And bring them cracking into the ravine
Like the three or four trees fallen and grown thin
And though not petrified, yet nevergreen:

Then put a friend on one extended shelf
Of rock at the top of the gorge, and let a fear
Shoot through you that an undertied shoelace
Will trip him and make him fall flat on his face
Two hundred feet, and, shuddering, at the bier
Of imagining make elegy for yourself.

FUN AND HOPE IN BRISTOL, ENGLAND

It was exciting, yes indeed, to quaff
Schooners of sherry drawn from wooden casks
In the port of Bristol — yes, and fun to dine
On *lasagna* and *vino da tavola*, red and white,
English and Americans, in a former wine
Cellar three or four hundred years old,
Celebrating out friends' wedding-to-be-in-two-days,
Calling for happiness, mostly for them,
Also for us — yes, and most fun to see
Bits of concrete fall from between the bricks
Of the low vaulted ceiling to a place
The fillings in my teeth ached to go too,
Then down, making her scratch the small of her
Dressed back beneath her near and nut brown shoulders.
"You'll be doing this some day," the bridesmaid I
Escorted whispered during Mendelssohn.
"I hope so," I said, and thought, *soon*, before
Sherry runs dry, neck sags, and all falls down.

SAGUARO

The saguaro grow so slowly they
    Do not reserve their succulence
    But sturdily give residence
To birds that otherwise would die.

Great cacti, with your black hole wounds,
    You are the crucifixion tale
    Enacted: that you seem to fail
Ensures for others healthy sounds.

In the great desert of the live
    We may observe this plant, and see
    That taking in what song may be
Helps stolid thirstlessness survive.

And, as birds talk their getting past
    Adversity in the living thing,
    Rodents and insects nearby sing
In a tripped saguaro that they last.

VIGNETTE

When the Queen Mary, the one time I was on her,
Called at Cherbourg, the way that skeletal hoist
Pincered the Cadillacs from Illinois
And packed them gently in the vessel's hold
Made me, observing its operator, think
Of drawing keen cartoons and smoking a pipe.

THE BEST PLACE TO READ CARLYLE

Where's the best place to read Carlyle? I'll tell you!
It's on a plank dock on Lake Webb in Maine,
Near Weld. You sit there in your trunks, in sun,
Reading Thomas in a 1700-thin-page
Anthology by Oxford, and when anything
Strikes you, you pencil in the margin, "Crux."
When bored, you dive into the lake. You surface
At the float, and lie on it. Sometimes you row
A boat a ways to a brook and silently
Flow up it in the hope of seeing beaver.
Before dinner, rye with ice chipped by a pick
From a 100-lb. block in a chest
That serves to keep food cold: Maryland rye,
Sipped in between bites of raw carrots. After,
Reading of other things by oil-lamp, or
Cards, or Double-Crostics. Often, talk.
Your host knows when to tell an anecdote.
Early to bed, not too late to rise, straight razor
For shaving in lake water. Near the end
Of every afternoon, a two-mile walk.
That is the only place to read Carlyle.

POST CARD FROM ESNA, EGYPT

*(CAIRO, Oct. 27 — Egyptian frontier
administration authorities said today that the police
still had not cleared up the identity of the body of an
American found in the Nubian Desert yesterday.*

    *Meanwhile desert patrols continued to search for
a second American in the ill-fated party that left
Aswan by motorcar July 26 headed for Waddi
Halfa on the Sudanese border.*

    *A three-week search by jeep, helicopter and
camel resulted yesterday in the finding of four
bodies in the lonely sands 275 miles south of
Aswan . . .*

    — The New York Times, Oct. 28, 1959)

Luxor and Edfu, Pyramids and Sphinx,
Port Said, Beirut, the Bosphorus, Paris,
Thus backward from the desert past Aswan
If lives were safety-film, at will rewound.
I take these place-names from the last post card
I have from my friend, John Armstrong. I could add
Orleans, Hong Kong, Manila, Monterey,
Cambridge, Amherst, and, interweaving all,
Preceding all, Belleville, New Jersey. But:
"Missent to North Chatham, Mass.," stamped in red ink.
No postmark on the UAR Egyptian stamps.
"July 24" in John's hand. At the end he says
"It is hot and dusty on the road, but now
We wait in Esna in the cool shade of trees
At the police station, waiting for a guide
To show us the way through the mountains to Aswan."
They got to Aswan, but not to Wadi Halfa
Across the Nubian Desert. Mysteries

Obscure the deaths of John and his three friends
Or two friends and an inexperienced guide.
"Their heroism lies on the other side
Of folly," says a spectator here in Texas.
"This was a serious fellow on a lark."
So: as Swift says, you should choose your moments well
For jumps into volcanoes: hero or fool,
Genius or madman, what thin lines! So: John was
Deadly serious along route 39
In throwing beercans at No Passing signs.
But I don't think John hoped for new answers, or
Was "in search of personal identity"
So avidly as to seek risk of death
In hope of revelation or some grail.
I think he expected to be alive today,
Translating Chinese into French. Just what
Happened, what monkey wrench cracked bloodily
Into what skull, what water spilled, what sun
Struck savage and incessant, what sands swept
Across what dimlit road, I do not know.
I have John's card, his hand: "No news from you,
A silence which has saddened me of late."
Then the names of places seen and to be seen.
I am saddened that I cannot ever break
My silence, which had saddened him of late,
And his full silence, which now saddens me.

BEDE

When the old thanes got drunk on sunny mead
And saw the swallow fly through the mead hall,
Did they send at once for the Venerable Bede,
Or was he there, imbibing bird and all?

He may have been the first offhand reporter,
Like many today, who rely for information
On dubious source, wire service, canned distorter,
Or he may have been someone used to distillation.

He was used to the Word of God. What word can be
More distilled, compacter, than "Let there be Light"?
Even if the bird flew when he couldn't see,
Mead to lips, eyes closed? or not there? Bede's mind shone
    bright

And said its quick flight, in and out, was the life of man.
However he got it, punditry began.

QUESTION

After the ecstasy, the ignorance.
The woman you just enjoyed and loved, a lump
Of unfamiliar and indifferent flesh.
The poem you read last night and experienced
As a flash of passionate vision, a dead page.
The Beethoven symphony, the Schubert song
Twinned in an eloquence, now separate.
After each thrust, the counter-thrust, disgust.
Yet out of each no, a yes... Yes, Stevens, yes!
But what of the sense that the complexity
Of what we do not know, and what we like
And taste, and little know, and what we love
And still do not much know, will baffle us?
That is the question, yes, that is the quest.

BEE

Life is very hard
For veneered egoists
Who fear finishes marred
By what resists

Their severe
Self-assertivenesses.
See, they go to the rear,
Thanks to wrong guesses

Instead of silences
That had meant "I don't know."
Violences
Come, viols go,

Till each scratched romantic,
Opinioned, cocky, sure,
Stands dull or stands frantic,
Battered, but pure.

WOOD

In this gray land the people are all wood
And would cry out, but icy is their bark.
They try to make their madness manifest
By writhing in the winds, but, understood
Senselessly, rooted in burnt frost, they rest
Till needed as the planks of a new ark.

Till the expected flood, they are the stock
Still stump people of a dumb wood world.
Time was most madmen had a gift of tongues.
Now men are mad and lumpish and like rock
That neither bleeds when torn nor has bright lungs
To blast out colors like a flag unfurled.

BESIDE THE SEA, IGNORANT MURDERER

I am separated from the ocean's roar
By something more sedate than any friend
Or I had reckoned on or bargained for:
Not distance, deafness: I am near, and hear it:
    Not indifference: I revere it:
But something in me like a dumb dead end.

The ocean roars: it pours its rage upon
The endlessly receptive shoals and sands
That are its mistress, orchestra, Verdun.
Lion, it loves the shore. Force, it ignores
    Life that itself abhors
The same as kelp, jellyfish, ampersands.

See there: a crowd has gathered round: the ocean
Threw up the corpse of one I knew who drowned
Knowingly, of his own meant lack of motion.
The rusty beer can near, the gray sopped spar
    And the dead body are
Equal as vomit, salty, seaweed-crowned.

Sing requiems, you standers-round, for Johnny,
Who sought out how it feels to be deceased
And found, but did not come and tell. His body
Sags soggy with the brine he swallowed when
    He swam far out, and men
Reached him when he had his life released.

Stomach, you cramp me, when I think of guts
In those like him, who risk what seems too much.
"Come in! the ocean's great!" I, in my ruts,

Take twenty minutes to get wet, explore
    Deeps very near the shore,
And inspect my inner dikes, just like the Dutch.

Now, is it that I am too self-contained?
I stand, and watch the crowd, and mourn the dead,
And hear the ocean roar, and am self-chained,
Perhaps by some idea of mastery,
    Perhaps an anti-sea,
Perhaps my essence, when all's done and said.

ANALYSIS

If the only way of giving up the past
Requires dexterity, I cannot do it.
I have lost too many fingers. At this last
I am not shoe enough. I do not rue it.

I know the amputating manners fail
To give affection, let alone full life,
To those who cut themselves that way from stale
Delights, with a not quite fully severing knife.

That is out of my questioning. I know the only
Way I can deal with my past is not to sever
The arteries that feed me, but, quite lonely,
To swallow the dead blood of dead endeavor.

I can and must make sure this dark ingestment
Clothes me and spangles me with bright investment.

ST. GEORGE, UTAH

Not the Gideon Bible, but the Book of Mormon
Sits gilt, in red-brown fabrikoid morocco,
On the table in my motel, named the Red Mesa.
I look about town, and I see the dragon
Slain only by the rape, for irrigation,
Of waters from the river, named the Virgin.
That thought should please old horny Brigham Young!
But the Virgin in Zion did so much erosion
It's only fair to use her to make fertile
Soil of some small part of the sandstone sands
And lava-spoors and limestone-leachings spread
As leavings for the sagebrush. Yes, St. George
Names well. It dominates southwestern Utah,
Thrusts human force against the lizard land,
Lances the living stream to stain the desert.
Its founding outcast cast away his past
And left no trail for hounding, cast his lot
Scentless against all chases, almost all
Fears, and most hopes. He was prepared to sow
Himself into a future. In his image
I see about me a fantastic forge,
A reason for Earth, an origin of myth,
And within and against this, dwarfed by it, St. George
Riding against . . .? against the word *Defeat*,
Waving aloft the sword Fecundity
In the name of seed, and harvest, and all good.

DOMESTIC SCENE AND ONE-LINE EPILOGUE

"You are coming apart," she says.
"Am I coming apart?" he asks.
"How am I coming apart?"
"Your shirt is out of your pants.
Tuck it in. You're coming apart."
"Oh, is that all you mean?
I thought you meant much more,
That I was coming apart."
"No, you're not coming apart,
Though sometimes I think you are."
"Oh, sometimes you think I am?
Then you did mean what you said."
"I meant only what I said."

"Granted," the judge says.

AN AMERICAN LIFE

The way the train burrows through West Virginia,
Making a way from Baltimore to Ohio,
From Chesapeake Bay to ravened El Dorado,

Is like the way a human life makes journey
From the bay of its birth into its own interior,
Finding itself its company all the way.

And it is a deception that its finding
Is of anything that it did not bring with it
As seed of an expected flourishing.

This is truest now, the past being our pastime,
When I go back through dead road gangs and tunnels
From gone-to west of Ohio to Baltimore,

And am reflexive, self bent back on self,
A life whose future likes its origins,
A road of rails ending where aim begins.

THOMAS HARDY

Hardy knew his genesis and numbers.
　　Leaning upon his coppice-gate,
He saw the iceberg and Titanic grow
　　　　Into their classic fate.

He took long views, tinted in somber umbers,
　　Dangerous old daguerrotypes,
Showing that time's tremendous force is slow
　　　　But brings to ground all snipes.

His verse was like the woodbine-lyres he sighted,
　　Gnarled, tough, and beautiful,
Aeolian harp-strings rusted by sharp wind
　　　　Or like a thrush-like gull.

Knowing no wrong, once done, is ever righted,
　　He stoically did few wrongs.
He thought of fate all while his face-flesh thinned,
　　　　And left six hundred songs.

T. S. ELIOT

Eliot saw much, thought he saw more:
Hair-shirt as summer underwear
Showed forth that he, like Everyman, bore
More than almost every man could bear,
Yet quietly, in what he wore.

He was the poets' astronaut:
He voyaged backward into Donne
And outward to a still point, thought
To be beyond, though like, our Sun,
And far past, though not unlike, Nought.

Yet, thank his dance, his stillest point
Flew like a locus into seas
And through backyards, making conjoint
Sweet peas with apotheoses,
Big Muddy with all blood anoint.

IN PRAISE OF M.B. TOLSON

M. B. Tolson is dead.
The writer of *Harlem Gallery* is dead.
He was sixty-six.
He should have lived longer.

He should have lived long as Stevens, Verdi, Chaplin.
He excluded nothing, nobody,
Except the repeatedly vain, repeatedly foolish,
And told them, excluding them, how to know better.

He loved life so much
That knowing him was almost to be his cancer,
Devouring him.
He and words were twins, at one.

In one of his favorite anecdotes
He told of a train delayedly stopping, a Frenchman getting off,
The Frenchman seeing his twelve-year-old paintings, the
    Frenchman asking him to come to Paris,
His mother barring the door for over a week thereafter.

That was how, he said, he turned to poetry.
He turned to it with great vengeance. He wrote words
He could say with tremendous power
And accuracy.

I remember Tolson, summer of '65,
Throwing a half-eaten McDonald's hamburger, in its paper,
    out the window
Of a moving car
And later describing that hamburger as white America.

And I remember M.B.,
The last time I talked with him, on the telephone,
Telling me to come see him,
Wherever, whenever,

At an impossibly imprecise time and place,
As if he knew his poems and life would soon end together
And he would not do all he wanted to do
And he wanted to talk about it: he wanted to talk.

He wanted to write the poem
Of negritude, the poem
Of human beings, happenstancedly black,
Of human beings.

Praise to Tolson now: he did
Less than he would, but more than at one
Time he may have thought he could do.
He was a poet.

RITES

Into an Argentine river, one young steer
Is driven bleeding, upstream from the ford
Where the herd will cross. Piranhas sense his blood
And in three minutes eat up all his flesh
In splashings, slashings, suckings, too obscene
To be inhumane. Lives leave the skull: the pain
In the glazing eyes, and then the eyes. All bones
Are slickly bare before the razors turn
Sated away, just as the last live steed
With its horseman reaches safety, having steered
The unsacrificed across.
                              High in Peru
People are dancing, brightly costumed, round
In lively patterns. At the right, felt time
A young man takes his partner from the throng
Without damage to the dance. They dash aside,
Then stop and breathe deep, smiling. Then the girl
Backs off, starts backing slowly from the man,
And he stalks her slowly, surely, along a path
Well-worn, to a waiting house. Her eyes show fear
And light, her smile says Stay away, Come on,
His face cannot be seen. In the open door
She pauses; she looks fine; her smile grows large
And he leaps, he leaps upon her. The door shuts.
The people dance the sun down and approve.

GUTS

A landscape hates the soul
Of its beholder, and,
Beholden to no one,
Can be a filthy hole,
An empty retch of sand,
A desolate Verdun.

It takes a man of hate
Hating the land right back
To take just what it gives:
A painter who makes mate
And lover of the smack
And stench of all that lives.

48

TACT

Oppositions to you can be angular
Or slithery: if you meet
A sure foe, be granular, be rectangular,
But to a slimy circular friend, be sweet!

Toughness appears in time, if it exists.
Snakiness disappears
As skins are shed, and no approach persists
Past its appeal to its particular fears.

You, as the one who sinks the ten-foot putt
That wins the whole team's match,
Know that not much now can be done to cut
You from your niche from out among the batch.

Yet you know people hate you. Who they are,
If you were someone other,
You would have spies to find. As you are, you spar
With your rough opponent as your softest brother.

THE ASSERTIONS

In this pool, antagonisms meet. The ledges
Show forth as specimens the bathing people.
The pool itself brims with a final water.
And when a person plunges in the pool
Wax melts, extremes meet, transiencies resolve
Into a moving stasis: in the flick
Of the opened lizard shutter of God's eye
The cleaving stroke of the swimmer, the cleft spray
Of the cloven surface and its tautened dancing
Are a caught tableau of opposites in tension:
The solid live wed to the liquid dead.
When George dove into the pool, and my eye caught
Him smashingly slashing ahead through the bright water
It was as if Kennedy had not died,
John Armstrong had not died in the Nubian Desert,
And I would not die: President, friend, I
Had nothing to do with any interruption
Of the assertions animate statues make
When they swim across a pool and do not drown.

LOVE SONNET

The special smell, of pines and deep decay,
    Wrapped itself round the cooking and the stove
    As if it were an emblem of all love:
The pining now, the long-since-pined-away.
Aster and disaster. Could I say
    Anything to you or anyone of
    The sudden new way I felt, above
All hopes I had had of today yesterday?

You were not here. Clearly you could not hear
    Any spring-fresh announcements I might make.
    Had you been here, still, still I very much doubt
    You would have understood what I had found out
    About the nature of love: that sudden take
Is give, you feed on the dead, and you play by ear.

LEGGIERO

After the hairs cover the feeble flesh
The thighs and even the calves seem more your own,
The not-so-fatted thighs and calves. But what
Hair-sock covers the naked anklebone?

You can make none. Lambs give you none. Down there
Laughter is silent, while around the vein
That always, as a child, intrigued you, new
Tiny offbleedings, beneath naming, skein

Your summer skin. And when your winter comes
They will stand out pronounced against the white.
You can do nothing to prevent this. Try,
While it is happening, to do hard things right.

Try to kiss your grandmother. Try not to kill
The tastes of youth tender within you still.

SELF-LOVER

Into a summer culvert the small boy
Crawls quietly. He stays there while he wants
The shadow, the dank odor, the weak husk
Of hollow water, and his separateness.
He is a universe beneath the road,
Cuddled complete, touching the top of his skull
To the concrete pipe, closing his eyes to feel
The flattening rush of tires rocket his head
Loose into spaces. Then, in deepest calm,
He takes himself alone within himself.
This is a unity beyond all words
Until his whole seems tiny, or stirs fear,
Or his shoulders ache. The far cylindrical light
Attracts him then, seems friendly. He crawls out,
Gathers his body, blinks, looks round, stands up,
Stretches, half-reaccepts the intricacy
Of living as a person on the earth.

LIE

I have no lie to tell
Other than one I know
You know too well:
How does it go?

"I have a sure sense
Of direction"? Do not smile.
Like mine, your excellence
Lies in that guile.

ON A PAINTING BY E. A. W. TEALL

Aunt Hannah waits. The little girls pick flowers.
The little girls are in their Sunday best.
The flowers the little girls pick are wild, my child.
Aunt Hannah waits up straight in a two-seat buckboard.
The road is two dirt ruts through grass. The horse
That pulls the buckboard stands dark, patiently.
The girls are white and blue, Aunt Hannah white,
Flowers white, red, grass yellow, green, hills blue.
No scent of carbon monoxide taints the air.
No car at any miles per hour, friend,
My child, has come, or will have gone away.
Two trees have fallen across the white stream.
Nothing is certain but destruction of trees
And death of blue and white little girls, the black
Horse, and Aunt Hannah: and, child, me, and thee.
No force outcertains change: child, see with me
The dozers bull a hell into this scene,
The damp white concretes harden on this canvas,
The diesels visually smell, the cars
Pump speed across and past the pastoral.
It could not last. My child, it did not last.
Here is what it was like. This depicts a past.
It shows going slow enough to pause, to stop,
Even on the way to Sunday school to pause
And take in bounty against any fast.

ECHO

My life depends on others': yet I pride
Myself on giving faithfullest service. When
Someone announces he is satisfied,
I tell him he is happiest of men.

When someone says he is dissatisfied,
I tell him gloom could not be more profound.
The only time my faculties are tried
Is when somebody's silence trumps my sound.

ON THE POPPING OUT OF EYES

Most people's eyes pop out one at a time
So they can use the one still in to find
The popped-out eye, and stuff it back in place
Before the one still in pops out. But some
Poor people have both eyes pop out at once.
What can they do? They scrabble on the ground
And frantically claw the earth. Some find
Their eyes, or one of them: sometimes one eye
Or both roll down the drain. And some get squashed.
It's a real problem, which Oedipus solved
In a way by using his thumbs the very split
Second he felt both eyes begin to pop.
Thanks for the remedy, Oedipus, but no thanks.
I'll try to keep my eyes like unpopped corn
By being amazed as seldom as I can
And looking at all things slightly askance.

PEARL HARBOR, 1976: AN AGONY AGAINST SUICIDE

Out of desperate non-knowledge what to do
I raise the dusty lid from the dusty keys
Of my upright piano, and play the first
Movement of a Beethoven sonata,
The one open, the twelfth, the noble 3/8 time
Four-square *Andante con Variazione*,
Out of desperate non-knowledge what to do
To help keep a friend from committing suicide
Out of a sense he has nothing to give others.
He likes fine music, has quick wit, loves words,
Values others' vivacities: why does he
Not prize his own? I think of one dead, who,
Out of desperate non-knowledge what to do
After too stodgy a year of graduate school,
Enlisted in the Army, learned Chinese
At Language School, Monterey, then from Manila
Leave-flew to Hong Kong to meet a cousin Scot
In the Royal Navy: by sheer will he got
Out of desperate non-knowledge what to do
And into the Sorbonne on a Fulbright, then
Died with three friends in what I take to have been
As assertive odyssey against time, through space,
Their way lost, in a desert. Their two motorcars
Fuse molten in sunburnt memorial.
Out of desperate non-knowledge what to do
For the living, I remember the close dead
And the distant dead of past time, remote space,
Whose fiery furnacing came close home into
Our Paper Mill Village livingroom the day
Thirty-five years ago exactly, when,
Out of desperate non-knowledge what to do

To rule passions, or people, let alone the world,
Nippon's rulers' bombers bombed our battleships
Moored at Pearl Harbor, and the radio noise
Came as too understandable static, making
The Philharmonic chaos. So, now, playing
Out of desperate non-knowledge what to do
To save a life, I celebrate those dead
Through any agency other than their own,
Passively, actively, however . . . Better
Keep going, die only unavoidably, try
Against time's foul cigar-smoked tooth-tear, than
Out of desperate non-knowledge what to do
To kill yourself. Better striver–deceiver,
Better sodomite-great metaphysical teacher,
Ulysses, Latini, than Pier delle Vigne.
Beethoven, join Dante, crying in deep sadness,
That he, the just, was to himself unjust,
Out of desperate non-knowledge what to do.

NOVEMBER IN TEXAS

Russets, rusts, burnt umbers, and charred greens:
These are the leaves of November in Texas. No
Oranges, yellows, reds. Shadings and sheens;
No clarities, no fires. The brilliant glow

Is not the leaves', here, but the bright blue sky's,
A crisping presence like a gasp of air,
A cloth of gold, a benison, a prize.
The sky is the true verdure, here. I stare

Into its sun-starred foliatedness
Amazed, and see a purity unlike
Maples and oaks froth-whipped within a stress
Of gale summering crost field-seas, yet like

That New England scene as ease is like unease.
The charred leaves chirr and rasp in the blue breeze.

LIME TOWN IN TEXAS

One or two miles around each lime
Plant I have seen the live oak trees
Are stunted if not snuffed out by
A coat of false perpetual snow.

Nearest the static rattling bomb
The fallout's thickest. People live
In clapboard houses caked with dust.
They may remember Mexico.

When the dusk Texas Eagle flies
At fifty-five or sixty through
The lime town, early diners see
Their fears of dentists laid out bare.

They see a set of mighty teeth
Ground into powder and then puffed
Upon the landscape by the cheeks
Of the inconstant shifting air.

RANCH ROAD 385

Was fine in the afternoon of November 2nd
Because the bright sun shone on the sheen of green
In the leaves of the stunted sideroad trees, and brought
Fire from the tips of the leaves the very last night's
Freezing air had barely nipped and reddened, and
A docile family of deer stood blending
On the left into the land of caliche crops,
Gnarled junipers, and tufts of bleached buff grasses,
And a single deer in the right roadside turned
Its tail and incredibly gracefully flowed as I slowed
Over a patch of the endless barbed wire fence,
And the road rolled, and distant mountain vistas
Appeared and were framed and unframed by shifting mesas
And my car gleamed rubiest red as it went forward
From above Mountain Home past Harper to under London.
Then clouds took hold, took over. Cautiously
Passing a Brahma bull stolidly standing
Broadside across my lane near the Llano River
(One side of most Cattle Guards one finds Loose Livestock),
I took dull roads toward home.

NEARING A JANUARY

That the train whistles in its dark
Makes my dark lighter, tenderer, less stark,
    For no sounder reason
Than that a friend who hinted suicide
  At Thanskgiving and who has not died
    Greets the Christmas season.

Iron horses and all flesh are as the grass.
  Thoroughbreds know this, therefore pass
    Through life with blooded measure:
  They sow songs as they go to seed,
Pour out blue rhythms as they breathe or breed,
    Give the airs haysmoke pleasure.

The diesel whistle I hear this midnight,
  Pallid, reflects in the pale eyes
    Of my visitor, my friend,
  A refused, admitted loss of size,
A tough and tenuous maintenance of the right
    Never to have to end.

LESSON

Which shell on the beach shall we take home? No matter.
All that shall not fade will be the remembrance
Stirred by the faded shell that all shells shone.

Put the brightest shell into your pocketbook, mother.
Engarland it with seaweedy encumbrance.
Crown the concoction with a glittering stone.

No matter that when we all get home, father
Quite rightly will I-told-you when the shell
Is dull, the seaweed shrunk, the stone but stone.

All laurels crumble, but they are small matter.
The shell and stone plainly remain, and well
Show that the watery flesh dries down to bone.

THE CHILDREN'S SNOW

The snow might stop, but then the shovelling
Must start in earnest. Better that it snow
Interminably, cover up the igloo,
Smother all contours of the land, smooth out
All life into one death, collapse the ice
Of the river by sheer pressure into stones
Of frozen water riving the bedded stones
Of the river into new shapes. Let contortion
Dominate wholly, clearness never come,
The snow continue, a white fall of grace
For all the country children who lie warm
In bed, and passionately do not wish
To contemplate rising, shovelling, going to school,
Doing anything at all. Let the snow go
On falling endlessly for the innocent sake
Of the children who spontaneously imagine
An end of the world under snow, but with each one
Of them somehow surviving, dominating,
Making parents and siblings toe their line, not heeding
The bullies who, turning out to be weaklings, freeze.
For the innocent? For the experienced sake
Of the country children let the snow not stop
Till, past the livingroom windows, it drift high
Against and over and past their bedroom windows
And atop the eaves, and cover the whole house.
That would be winter indeed! for them, a winter
Equal to their intense desire for snow
Overwhelming their enemies, actual, potential,
Releasing them from claims, a snow of great
White endless anti-shovelling falling down,
Anti-school, anti-getting up, anti-anti-freeze,
A knowing snow, suckling them in their dreams
Of power in the world of aftersnow.

NOVEMBER 25, 1963

The assassination of the President,
Among its many effects, confers upon
The slightest act a clarity of precision.
The sharpening of a pencil with a knife,
My old Scout knife, twenty years old, today
Sharply reseen as its invented self.
The cutting of my nails with old small scissors,
Trying, as always, not to hurt the quick.
Then encountering, taking up the pencil,
Tooth marks, not mine, and breaking it in half
In the frustration of rage, despair, and grief
At life not being as it ought to be.
She bit it. Our love should be alive, as he
Much more should be, and stupidly is not.

SHILOH: THE BLOODY POND

At Shiloh, Tennessee, a finite number
Of days after the first day's bloody fighting,
To be exact, thirty-six thousand, nine hundred
And forty-nine, two, three, or four generations
As parents and children go, I mourned the dead
And the unsown seed of those who left no orphans,
And mystically felt, in a time foreshortened
By the triangular presence in that Park
Of a National Cemetery, of covered trenches
For Southern dead, and of Indian burial mounds
From a million days before our Union shivered,
That if I knelt and drank from the Bloody Pond
I would taste the intermingled corpuscles
Of the thirsting Federal and Confederate dead.

LAKE WINDERMERE, JULY 10, 1967

Having entrained today to Windermere
From thirteen straight days of hecticity
In the great London, I am seeking here
    Wordsworth's passivity.

Gazing out on the lake from my inn room,
I hear the sounds of motorboat and bird —
Chirper, gull, raucouser — and, through bright gloom
    See, calmly stirred,

Beyond a midge-cloud, a lone sailboat glide,
Then see and hear a rowboat, two forms rowing,
One form a shroud, going against no tide,
    With no tide flowing,

Then let my eyes outfocus from those three
In one, onto a dark green wall of ore,
Falling, a lush deep carpeting, to be
    The water's floor

And surface, merging things, making them one
Another's. Noises come from behind the doored hall
Into the back of my head, and lightly stun
    Me with human call:

A nearby woman, saying to a man,
"You can use my bath," and him accepting; near
The distant shaft, small children. Good. They can
    Not interfere

With the encouraging happening here now.
They must join in. I gently will them, Come
Into the peacefulness I have, allow
    Me to make quick home

In me for you and all your history.
Love is obscure and many: ends, begin:
Passenger, rowers, all, be mystery:
    They do join in.

ACQ2488

2/9/94
gfa

PS
3573
H45
W45
1982